# F-SHARK
## Book 1

by Daniel Webster

Clifton Green Publishing

All original pieces and illustrations by Daniel Webster © 2022

www.fshark.co.uk

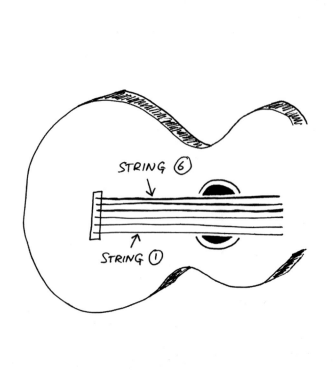

STRING ⑥

STRING ①

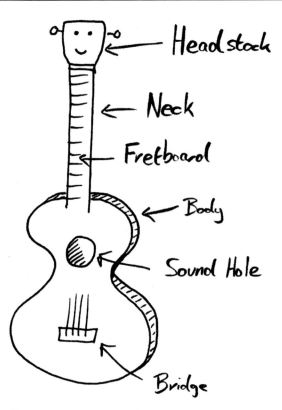

Headstock

Neck

Fretboard

Body

Sound Hole

Bridge

Left Hand

Right Hand

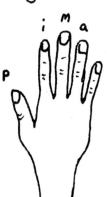

## How to play 'Free Stroke'

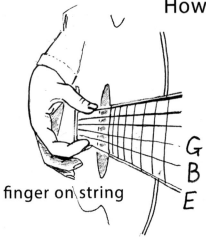

finger on string

G
B
E

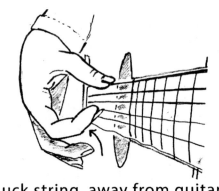

pluck string, away from guitar

2

# First Three Notes

STRING ①     STRING ②     STRING ③

**E**     **B**     **G**

## Walking Fingers

i m i m    i m i m...

## LIGHTNING BOLT

i m i    m i m ...

1 2 3 4

1 2 3 4

NOTE LENGTHS

$\{$

♩ = Crotchet (1 Beat)

𝅗𝅥 = Minim (2 beats)

𝅝 = Semibreve (4 beats)

**New Time Signature:**

$\frac{3}{4}$ means there are 3 crotchet beats in every bar.

Tap this rhythm:

# Dracula's Castle

## Notes on String ②

B — open
C — fret 1
D — fret 3

D ← 3
C ← 1
Left Hand

# SPACE WALK

STRING ①

$\hat{E}$  $\hat{G}$  $\hat{A}$  $\hat{B}$  $\hat{E}$

open    fret 3    fret 5    fret 7    fret 12

ALIEN INVASION

i m i m M...

5

7

12

7

5

⭐ All these notes are on String 1 - follow the fret numbers and try to learn the note names

# Quazy Quavers

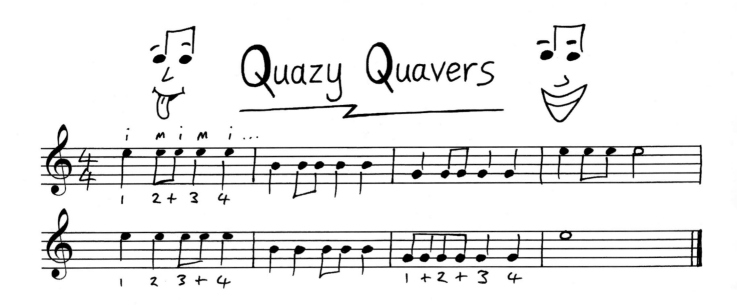

Quavers : ♫ or ♫

One Quaver : ♪ or ♪

A quaver lasts for half the length of a crotchet - so there are 2 to every beat

Clap : $\frac{4}{4}$  CROTCHETS  |  QUAVERS
1  2  3  4  |  1 + 2 + 3 + 4 +

# Chilli Pepper

Play this as a solo piece or go to page 20 to turn this into a duet or a trio

**Rhythm**

count : ♫ ♪ ♫ ♪ ♪
1 +(2) + 3  4

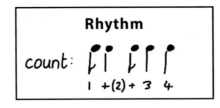

Play this piece as a duet with another guitarist - try playing both guitar 1 and Guitar 2

**Notes on string ③**

String ③ — **A** — fret 2

String ③ — **G** — open

SALAMANDER SAMBA

String ③

'Tie'

A _tie_ joins two notes together
play the first note then keep it going for the second.

# SUPER HEDGEHOG

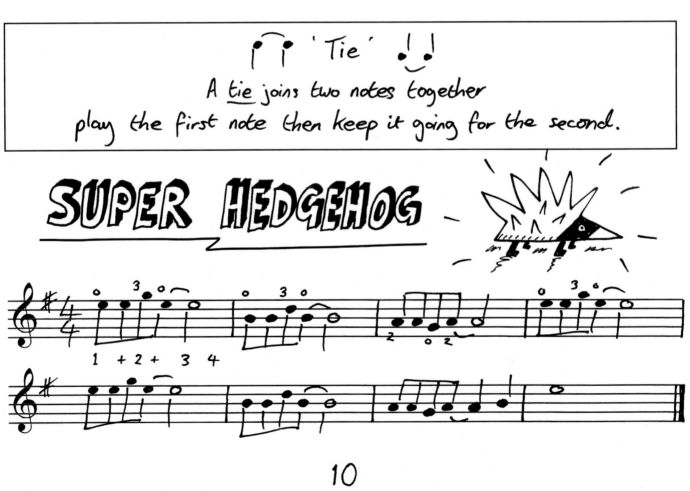

1 + 2 + 3 4

# mangoes AND coconuts

# ROBOT DANCE

⭐ If you haven't already, try this piece using 'rest stroke'

# Firefly

Notes you need:

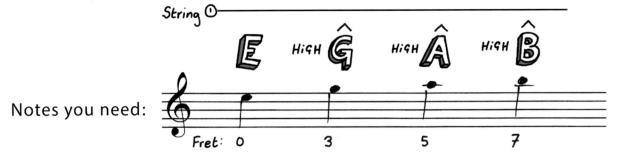

String ①

E    HIGH Ĝ    HIGH Â    HIGH B̂

Fret:   0        3        5        7

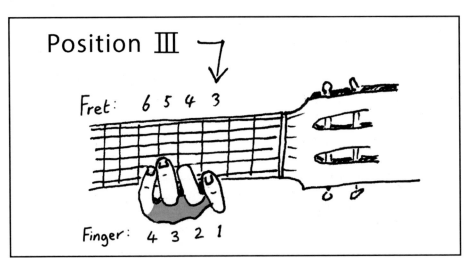

## Position III

Fret:  6  5  4  3

Finger:  4  3  2  1

12

# Jingle Bells

New rhythm: ♩. = Dotted Crotchet ( 1½ Beats )

---

**Alternate Endings:**

1. _____  First time bar (with repeat)

2. _____  Second time bar

---

# Sur le Pont d'Avignon

15th Century French Dance

notes you know:

| ① | | | ② | | | ③ | |
|---|---|---|---|---|---|---|---|
| E | F | Ĝ | B | C | D | G | A |
| 0 | 1 | 3 | 0 | 1 | 3 | 0 | 2 |

13

# CHORDS

A CHORD is 2 or more strings played together

x x x o o

O = Open String

x = Don't play this string

●3

Press finger 3 on here

# MINI CHORDS

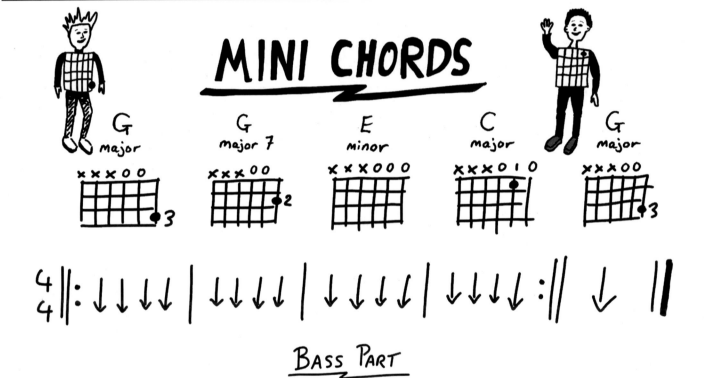

| G major | G major 7 | E minor | C major | G major |
|---------|-----------|---------|---------|---------|
| x x x o o | x x x o o | x x x o o o | x x x o 1 o | x x x o o |
| ●3 | ●2 | | ● | ●3 |

## BASS PART

STRING ⑥ — — — — — ⑤ — — — — — repeat

fret: 3      7      7      3      3

✸ Add the bass part to turn this piece into a duet

↓ = Down Strum

Play all the strings in the chord with thumb, back of fingernail or pick

14

# Duet
# AIRSHIP

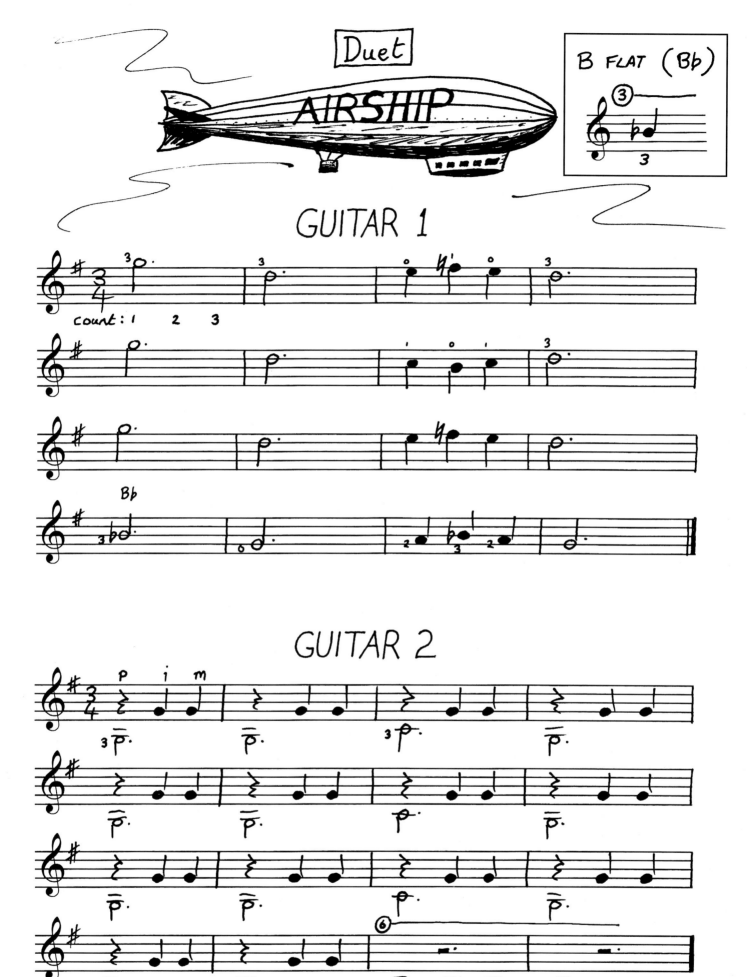

These two pieces make a duet when played at the same time. **Guitar 1** is the *pupil's* part, **Guitar 2** is the *accompaniment*

Accomp : ‖ G | G | C | D | G | G | D | G ‖

16

# Burning Down The Track

This is easier than it looks. Just follow the fret numbers for now.

17

# WOOLLY MAMMOTH

ALL ON STRING ⑥

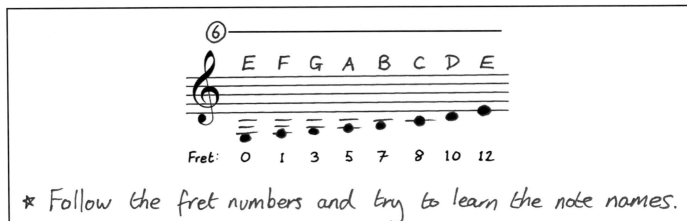

* Follow the fret numbers and try to learn the note names.

⌢ is a pause or 'fermata'

## penguins

★ Play this 'arpeggio-style': let all the notes ring together

### Key Signature:

When a sharp or flat (# or ♭) is written just after the clef, this is a **KEY SIGNATURE**. All the **F**s in this piece become **F#**
The key of this piece is **G major**

# SURF GUITAR

*Also try playing this piece with a pick

---

NEW TIME SIGNATURE: $\frac{6}{8}$ = 6 Quavers in each bar

---

# Pirates Ahoy

Play **Guitar 1** and **2** together for a duet; add **Guitar 3** for a trio

# NOTE LENGTHS

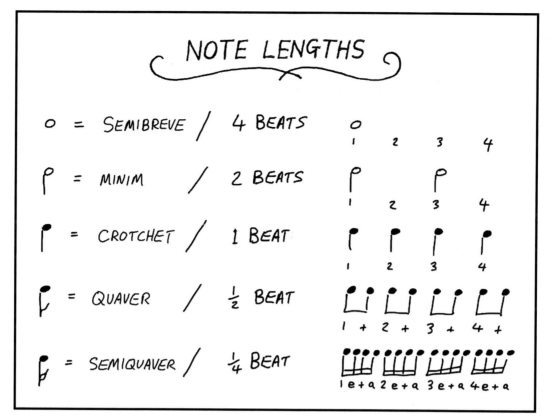

o = SEMIBREVE / 4 BEATS

𝖕 = MINIM / 2 BEATS

𝖕 = CROTCHET / 1 BEAT

𝖕 = QUAVER / ½ BEAT

𝖕 = SEMIQUAVER / ¼ BEAT

## The Stave

Treble Clef

## Notes on the LINES

E    G    B    D    F

## Notes in the SPACES

F  A  C  E   ☺

## DYNAMICS

*pp* = *pianissimo* (VERY QUIET)

*p* = *piano* (QUIET)

*mp* = *mezzo piano* (MODERATELY QUIET)

*mf* = *mezzo forte* (MODERATELY LOUD)

*f* = *forte* (LOUD)

*ff* = *fortissimo* (VERY LOUD)

Get **F SHARK Book 2** to
continue the adventure...

16120403R00015